THE FIRST BOOK OF
WATER

AF589611

This edition published 2023
by Living Book Press

ISBN: 978-1-922950-69-7 (hardcover)
978-1-922950-68-0 (softcover)

This edition Copyright © 2023 Living Book Press

All rights reserved. No part of this publication may be reproduced, stored in a retrieval system, or transmitted in any other form or means – electronic, mechanical, photocopying, recording or otherwise, without the prior permission of the copyright owner and the publisher or as provided by Australian law.

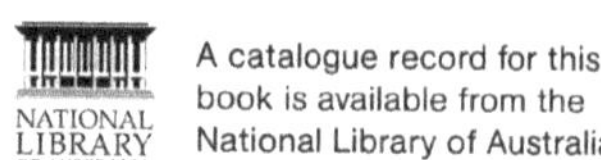

A catalogue record for this book is available from the National Library of Australia

THE FIRST BOOK OF WATER

Written and illustrated by

Jo *and* Ernest Norling

NOW HERE, NOW THERE !

Water seems to have magic. Here it is and now it's gone! You see it and now you don't! It is water—now vapor—now a cloud! It falls from the sky! It's a pool on the ground! Now it's gone again! It runs down the river but the river is still full! It pours steadily into the great ocean, but the ocean never runs over! It appears at dawn as shiny drops of dew on the grass. Look again later and presto, the drops are gone! Now it has changed from a drop of water into a snow crystal! It's a piece of ice you can hold in your hand for a minute gone now, dripping through your fingers!

What is this water that keeps changing and moving about? We believe that many ages ago a piece of sun was thrown so far out into space that it formed a new planet we call Earth. As Earth cooled, two kinds of gases united to make water. One of these gases is hydrogen. It is so light in weight that it is used to fill balloons so that they may rise high above the ground. The other gas is oxygen. Airmen carry tanks of it when they fly high into the stratosphere, for no one can stay alive where oxygen for breathing is scarce.

The Master Magician-The Sun.

Chemists tell us that these two gases united in a certain way make water. They write water "H_2O" to show that it is made of twice as much hydrogen as oxygen. Water is without color, although a large amount of it often reflects the color of the sky and shore. If there is any taste or odor, it belongs to something the water carries and not to the water itself. Water is tasteless!

ON THE TOP AND UNDERNEATH

Water flows downward until stopped by something in its way. Then it spreads out, creeping into all the lowest places, until it finds a new path down or becomes high enough to flow over whatever is blocking its way. This spread-out water may be a small pool or a large lake, but

its surface is flat and is called the water level.

Water poured into a watering can fills up the spout to the same level as that in the main part of the can.

A fountain supplied with water from a tank will shoot up almost as high in the air as the water level in the tank.

When Mr. Smith dug his well, the water came out of the ground like a fountain. He called it a "flowing well" because the water didn't have to be pumped up. A friend told him that such a well is called an artesian well. He said that its water comes underground from a higher point and is trying to reach its water level.

Water does not seem to be a bit solid, because you can dip your hand in it with hardly any effort, but its surface is held together by a force called surface tension.

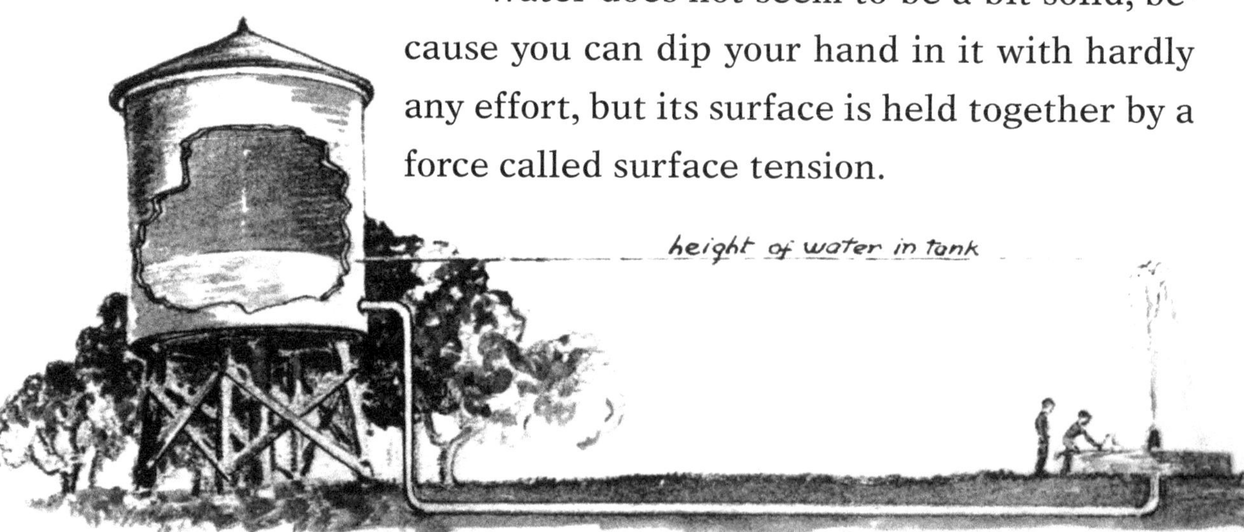

When you are learning to dive you know how a "belly flop" stings, so you practice in order to learn to hold your body correctly. A high diver knows that the water isn't as easy to break into as it appears. When he strikes the surface at a high speed the water doesn't part as quickly as he wishes, so he holds his hands to form a cutting edge to break the surface. His head and body follow through.

Some waterbugs stride about over this water surface as if it were ice. If you are very careful you can float a dry needle on the surface of water and you can see where the weight of the needle bends the surface down without breaking through.

Shake your hand in water, and air bubbles form. It is surface tension that holds the film of water around the little balls of air.

Water has buoyancy—an upward push. It can float anything on it that weighs less than the water that it displaces. Freddie's rubber boat weighs seventy-five pounds.

It is packed into a tight square bundle one foot high. A square bundle of water one foot high weighs sixty-two pounds. If Freddie put his packed boat in water it would sink because it is heavier than the same amount of water. But Freddie blows up his boat until it becomes twenty times bigger. It still weighs seventy-five pounds, while the water it displaces weighs over half a ton. Now it floats easily and carries Freddie and as many of his friends as can find room inside.

The steel used to build a battleship weighs thousands of tons and would sink if it were in one bundle. Built into a ship, it weighs less than a water battleship the same size, so it floats.

Your body is a little heavier than the water it displaces, but you can float if you keep your nose above water for breathing and help a bit by pushing with your feet and hands.

Salt water is heavier than fresh water, so you find it easier to float in the ocean than in rivers and lakes.

If you want to see for yourself that salt water has more buoyancy than fresh water, just put an egg into a glass of water. The egg will sink to the bottom. Now stir in two tablespoonfuls of salt and watch the egg rise and float.

Try another experiment. Take three glasses and fill each one part full of water. Drop a chip of wood into the first glass. It will float and keep on floating unless, after a longer time than you will care to wait, it becomes so water-soaked that it is heavy enough to sink. Old logs and boards that have stayed in the water for years now lie under water.

Into the second glass of water stir a spoonful of dirt. As long as you stir it to keep the water moving, the dirt is mixed throughout the liquid but not dissolved. Scientists say it is carried in suspension. Let the water stand quietly and the dirt is dropped to the bottom.

Into the third glass stir a little salt and sugar. They will dissolve and stay dissolved even though the water is quiet. Scientists say they are carried in solution. If you pour out the water, the sugar and salt go with it. But if you let the glass stand in a warm, sunny place, the water will evaporate, leaving the sugar and salt mixed in the bottom of the glass. In this way water dissolves and mixes many substances.

Water carries many things. It floats objects on its surface as it does logs. It carries particles of material in suspension as it does dirt. It carries minerals, such as salt, in solution.

WATER IS IMPORTANT

You have only to look about you to see all sorts of objects that are made with water. The paper in this book was made from a tree that used many gallons of water a day while it was growing. Thousands of gallons more were used at the mill to reduce the tree to pulp and make paper.

All living things are part water. You, yourself, are more than two-thirds water. It is all through your body, keeping you moist and regulating your temperature so that you do not become too hot. As a part of your blood stream, water carries materials and food necessary to repair your worn parts and add to your growth. And water carries off your body wastes.

Water is important to our everyday life. The turn of a tap brings it into our bathrooms, kitchens and laundries. We wash with it. We cook with it. We drink it.

The hydrant, out there in the street, stands ready to spout its water onto a burning house or to fill the sprinkler's water tank so that it may wash down the city streets. Father is putting water in the radiator of his car. A neighbor uses her hose to water her lawn. Across the street, men hose water into plaster for the walls of a new house.

WATER IS A TRAVELER

All this water comes from pipes where it has been imprisoned and led to our homes, but before that, it may have traveled around the world. It might have been almost anywhere. Water is on top of the ground. It runs down from the high places of the earth as tumbling streams. It flows in valleys as rivers. It fills hollows with lakes and has made great oceans. Frozen, it lies as ice and snow on the earth's always cold polar regions and on its highest mountain peaks.

Water is underground. It percolates through the soil, filling the cracks in rocks and the spaces in layers of gravel. It drips into caverns, where it becomes underground lakes and rivers.

IT'S RAINING

Water is all around us. It never stops traveling. Heated by the sun, billions of tiny drops keep rising from the ocean as invisible gas, called vapor, pushing and crowding to get higher and higher into the air. From the land as well as from the ocean, water vapor is rising. It comes from the rivers, the lakes, the little pools, the wet ground, your skin, a washing on the line. From these and all other water surfaces the sun with the help of the wind is evaporating water and whisking it away to join the ocean vapor in the air. Usually you do not see water leave, but if the air is cooler than the water the vapor may condense slightly, and you will see it rising like steam from wet places.

Far above, where the air is cooler, billions of these tiny drops of vapor cling together in visible masses and travel as clouds across the sky. When a rain cloud travels into cold air, the vapor drops cool even more and go together to form drops of water. Too heavy to stay up there

any longer, they come falling to earth. Then someone says, "It's raining."

"It's raining!" Virginia says as she stands at the window, wishing that the rain would go away and never come back. She wants to play with the kittens on the grass. She doesn't know how important water is—that without it all living things would dry up and die. Why, without water there could be no kittens, no grass, no Virginia herself!

Johnnie doesn't know this either, but he knows that water is fun! With raincoat, cap and boots on, he sails his little boats down the stream the rain is making in the gutter as it runs down the street on its way to the drain. He likes to swim in the lake near his home or play on the ocean beach during summer vacation. He can have fun playing

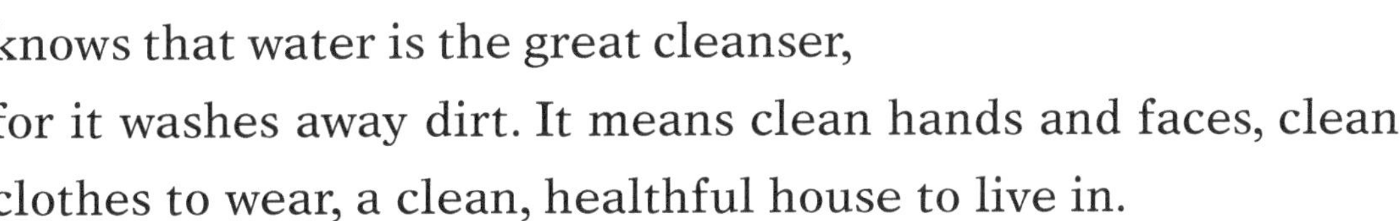

with the hose right in his own yard. Johnnie even likes to take a bath! "Water is such fun!" he says. Mother says, "The rain will wash the dust from the streets and the air. How nice everything will smell!" Mother never could do her work without water. She knows that water is the great cleanser, for it washes away dirt. It means clean hands and faces, clean clothes to wear, a clean, healthful house to live in.

Father works for the city water department. He knows that during a long dry spell people use a great deal of water from their taps to water their gardens and lawns. They draw from the city reservoirs more water than can flow in to keep them filled. Half-empty reservoirs mean city water rationing. "Good thing, this rain!" Father says. "We won't have to ration water now!"

Sister Sue doesn't want the rain to go away, but she wishes the rain cloud would meet such cold air that the drops would freeze and fall as snow. Sue can hardly wait for winter to come so that she can ski.

Big brother Bob thinks, "Some of this rain may run clear to the ocean. We've got to keep that ocean full because some day I'm going to float my own big ship there." Bob knows that the ocean is a great wide highway for ships to carry people and cargo to all the countries of the world. Water is a very important part of his dream of what he is going to do when he is a man.

Mr. Larson is a hydro-electric engineer. To him, water is power for generating electricity. "Why, electricity does most of our work these days," he says. "Just push in a plug or turn a switch and without even saying one magic word, you have light, heat or power to run anything from a toy train to a big locomotive that will pull a hundred cars full of freight." Mr. Larson knows that plenty of

water is needed behind the high dam at the lake if the city is to have more and cheaper electricity.

The farmer, looking over his fields, can see the wilting leaves of his corn freshen as the rain seeps into the dry earth. He knows that the rain water is carrying minerals from the soil into the corn's tiny rootlets and up through their stems into the leaves. "There'll be a good crop, after all," the farmer thinks. Good crops mean good things to eat for his family, farm animals, and for the people in the cities who depend upon him for their food.

Away up in the mountains, the ranger who takes care of a national forest sees the rain with thankful eyes. For weeks no rain has fallen. The evergreen trees of the forest have become so dry that they could burn easily and fast. The ranger's helpers have had to stay day and night in their lookout stations on the high peaks to watch for and report any rising smoke that

would show a fire has started. Fighting a forest fire is very hard and dangerous work, and vast areas of trees might be burned before the fire could be put out. Now the rain is dripping from the branches of the trees onto the brush below. The forest is safe again!

From under the forest trees the rain water trickles into little streamlets that flow into larger streams that join together to make rivers. Into lakes and out again these rivers may go—always taking the easiest way down—going slower now through the wide valleys until they finally reach the ocean. Here they can go no farther, for they have reached the lowest place they can, out of which a river cannot flow.

Not all of the rain that falls runs away to the ocean. Much of it goes into the ground, sinking as far as it can.

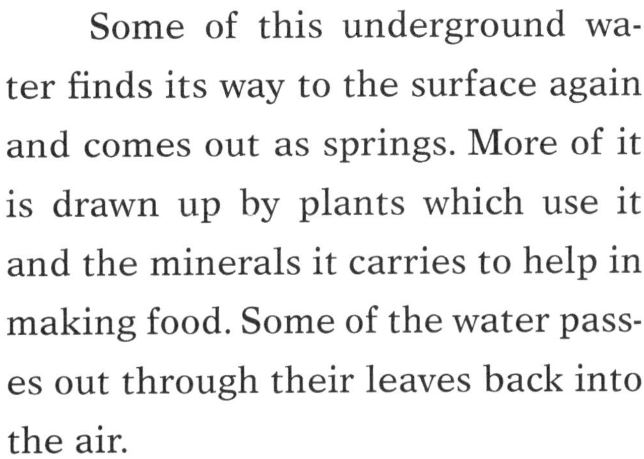

Some of this underground water finds its way to the surface again and comes out as springs. More of it is drawn up by plants which use it and the minerals it carries to help in making food. Some of the water passes out through their leaves back into the air.

WATER AND WEATHER

Water never stops traveling and it also changes form. If the temperature of the water falls below 32 degrees Fahrenheit, it freezes and becomes solid ice. If the temperature

rises to 212 degrees Fahrenheit, water at sea level boils and goes skipping off into the surrounding air as vapor.

When water freezes it expands — grows larger — taking up just a little more room than it did before. This allows ice to float on the surface of a lake instead of sinking to the bottom.

Water expands, too, when it becomes vapor, but then it expands to great distances. A spoonful of water can quickly fill a space as large as a room with water vapor, and the warmer it gets, the faster and farther and higher it spreads. Water vapor from boiling water is called steam.

When a rain cloud enters freezing cold air, its vapor drops form crystals and fall as snow. If the temperature at the ground is also freezing, the snow piles up and stays until the temperature rises and melts it. Sometimes snow is dry and squeaky under our feet when we walk on it, and it blows easily before a wind into little hills we call snowdrifts. But if the air is warmer, the snow is wet and packs readily into snowballs. Snow crystals are beautiful. Look at them through a magnifying glass, and you will see that most of them have six points but that no two of them ever seem to be exactly alike.

The churned-up air around a thunderstorm may catch the raindrops falling from a cloud and toss them back and forth from warm air to cold air several times before they fall to the earth as balls of ice. These hailstones are usually no bigger than marbles, but have been known to be as large as tennis balls. It is fortunate that hailstorms do not come often and that they are over quickly, for they can do much damage to trees, buildings, and even people.

When droplets of water, tiny but big enough to see, fall so slowly seem to be staying in the air, we have mist.

Sometimes we have fog. If you want to know how it would feel to be in a rain cloud, just go for a walk on a very foggy day, for is really a rain cloud close to the ground.

When plants, stones and other surfaces become cooled, as they usually do at night, the water vapor in the air that touches them also becomes cooled and condenses on them into drops of water. Then people say, "The dew has fallen!" although it doesn't really fall at all. If surfaces are freezing cold,

the vapor freezes into crystals and we have frost instead of dew. Frost crystals sometimes spread on a window in such a way that they look like trees, plants, or even animals and people.

You have watched clouds and perhaps said, "See, that cloud looks like a horse! Now it looks like a dog! Now it looks like a duck!" So you know that clouds, too, keep changing. They grow larger or smaller, sometimes disappearing entirely or forming before your eyes in a clear sky.

Running water works and the faster it runs and the farther it falls, the more work it does.

Perhaps you have seen the Grand Canyon, which the

Colorado River cut deep into the earth. Perhaps you live near the great delta of land that was built up with dirt carried out into the ocean by the Mississippi River, or you have made a trip to Niagara Falls, where the water has cut the falls back through rock.

These are famous examples of the wearing away by water, called erosion, that has been going on for a long period of time. In the same way, streams everywhere are cutting into the earth and carrying parts of it away. Swift streams wash dirt and gravel down mountain slopes as they dig deeper and deeper into the mountain itself. They tear rock apart and roll pieces of it along. They snatch soil from their banks as they hurry by and carry it with them to drop in quieter water, farther along.

The fine earth that streams pick up, carry along and drop is called silt. Many choice valley farmlands were once lakes—but flowing streams gradually filled them with silt.

Water dissolves minerals from the rocks and soil of the land through which it travels. It carries these minerals in solution wherever it flows. But when it takes off into the air as water vapor, it leaves them all behind. Ocean water carries such large quantities of mineral salts in solution that it is not fit for us to drink. If you were adrift in a boat with ocean water all around, you would still need to catch enough fresh rain water to keep you alive!

Ocean water, influenced by the sun and the moon and the wind, also travels and works. Currents of water move like riv-

ers through the ocean. Tides rise and fall so that the beach of wet sand you walked on this morning is covered with ocean later in the day. The waves beat upon the land, breaking down cliffs, filling bays with dirt and gravel, and building sandbars.

Water works, too, when it freezes into ice, for it pushes out to make more room for itself. On some very cold morning you may find the bottles of milk sitting on the porch with their caps pushed out by long necks of ice. If a cover had been screwed on tightly, the ice would have broken the bottle in order to get out. Water freezing in deep cracks in rock pushes the rock apart. Water freezing in wet ground may push heavy boulders

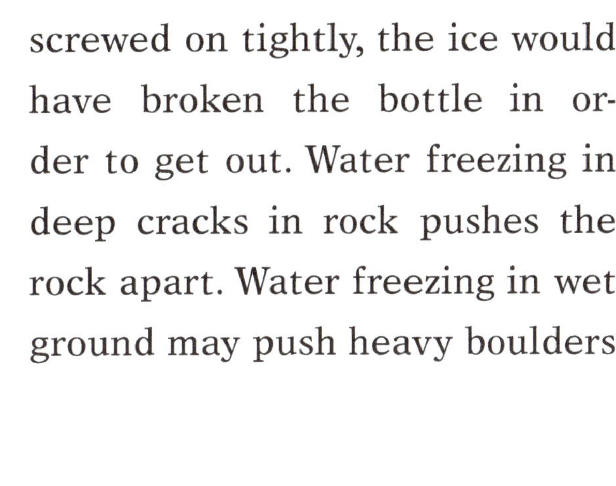

up from the ground and send them rolling and thundering down hillsides.

High mountain peaks receive snow both winter and summer. The fallen snow piles up so high that its own weight packs it into hard glacial ice and pushes it very slowly down the mountain. All the while the upper ends of these glaciers are building up with snow, the lower ends are melting and running away as rivers.

Glaciers move so slowly that they seem not to move at all, but mountain climbers who cross them say that there is a cracking sound as the ice shifts along. Sometimes cracks that are hundreds of feet deep open in the ice and later close again. These great masses of moving ice gouge out pieces of rock from mountains and grind them into boulders which they leave pushed into piles at their melting ends.

DESERTS, SWAMPS AND IN BETWEEN

While water may be almost anywhere, it is more plentiful in some places than in others. The greatest amount is in the oceans which join together to make one really large ocean that covers almost three-fourths of the earth.

Another amount of water is locked in the ice that covers the polar regions. On Greenland this ice cap is over one thousand feet deep in many places.

There are swamps where the water is not deep but never entirely runs off.

There are warm jungles where so much rain falls that trees and vines grow close together, forcing men to cut a path through them if they wish to pass.

The desert is quite different. There rain almost never falls.

Any water that might be in the ground is too far down for men to reach. Over most of the driest deserts even plants cannot reach water, so there are no growing roots to keep the sand from shifting about in the winds. Men who wish to ride and carry goods across the great deserts of Africa and Asia use camels instead of horses. Camels can walk easily in the soft sand; they can close their nostrils during sandstorms; and most important of all, they can store enough water in stomach pouches to last them several days. These long camel caravans will sometimes go miles out of their way just to get to a water hole where some underground water has come to the surface.

Some lands called arid or semi-arid get little rainfall, or are dry for parts of the year. Here plants send their roots far into the ground, grow smaller above ground, and often store water in their leaves and stems.

Perhaps you live where the amount of water seems just right, where trees grow and where rain falls just often enough to water the farmers' growing crops. But even in such a fine place you sometimes hear people talk of dry seasons and wet seasons and what to do about them.

Water is so important to people that they must live where they can get it. For thousands of years they had to live where water was found on or near the top of the ground. If the stream

or lake or spring dried up, they had to go somewhere else to live, near water.

When they first learned to bring water from deeper underground, they hoisted it in jars and buckets. Later they learned to pump it to the surface. People pumped water by hand, they made animals pump for them, and they put the wind to work. In modern times, engines and motors pump for us, but hand pumps and windmills are still used. Watch for them when you drive in the country. Sometimes you will see a windmill far out in a field, pumping water for cattle and horses to drink.

Water may be pumped as it is needed or piped from storage tanks.

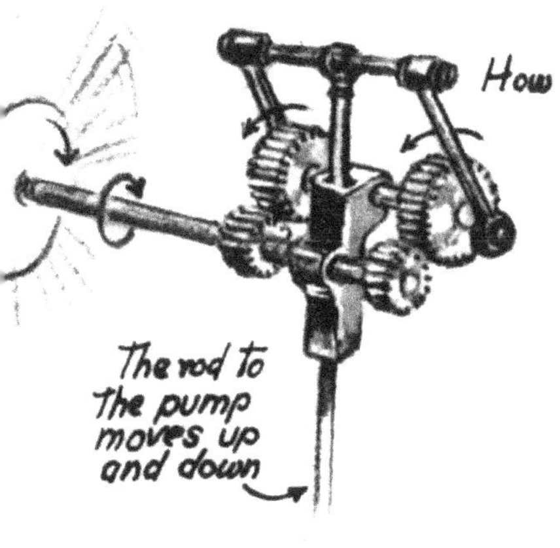

COLLECTING WATER

Many people like to live near one another in towns and cities. But a city can grow large only if its people are sure of enough water for their needs. They must be sure, too, that their drinking water is pure.

Water often has to be piped quite a distance from a lake or stream and sometimes from a spring or well. The city of New York gathers water from many streams. Chicago's water is pumped out of Lake Michigan through pipes tunneled miles out from shore. Some of Los Angeles' water supply comes 250 miles across mountains from the melting snows of Mount Whitney. Another supply from the Colorado River comes all the way across the state of California.

The people of ancient Rome brought their water across the hills in high stone aqueducts that bridged across valleys and canyons. Our modern aqueducts carry water across the floors of valleys instead of bridging them, and they even carry water under river beds in huge iron pipes.

When the water flowing through the aqueduct reaches a city, it is stored in tanks or in lakes called reservoirs. Fresh water flows into the reservoirs constantly, and care is taken to keep it fresh and pure. It is strained and filtered, and often helpful chemicals are added to kill harmful germs that might

get into the water supply before it reaches the tap in your home.

Reservoirs are usually built on hills so that water runs easily from them to the houses they serve. If there are no hills, water storage tanks are raised high by putting them on stilts.

Often water supplies are made larger by building dams across streams so that water cannot pass until it reaches a higher level. Dams spread rivers into lakes or lakes into larger lakes, and increase the amount of stored water.

Dams are often built to collect water for use on arid lands. Gates in the dams hold back the abundant rains and melted snows of the wet season. When the gates are opened during the hot, dry season they let the stored water flow into pipelines. The pipelines carry the water along the valleys so that each farmer can ditch some onto his own land and let it run over his fields and gardens.

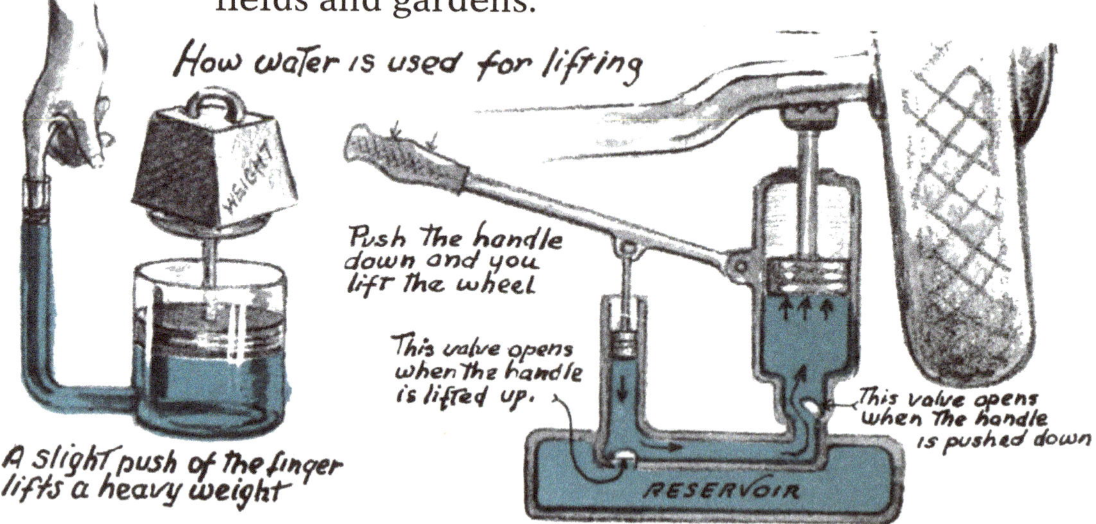

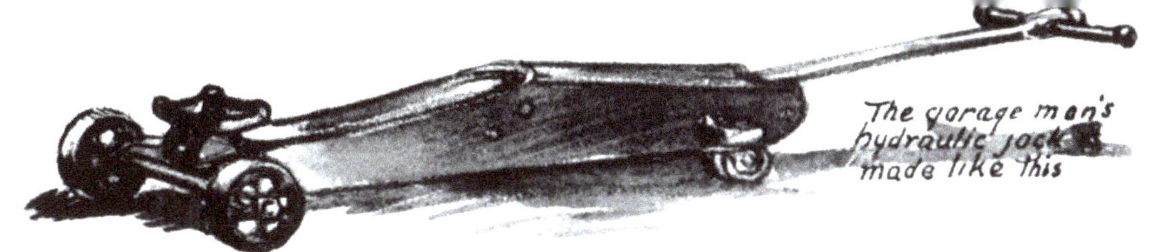

Once upon a time, someone, noticing the push of falling water, must have said to himself, "Why not let water work for me?" Perhaps the first water wheel he made was as simple as the one you might make by putting together two flat sticks, but he soon must have seen that more blades in his wheel gave more power.

A water wheel is placed in a waterfall in such a position that the falling water hits upon the blades of the wheel and turns it around. If the water falls on the blades from above, the wheel is called an overshot water wheel. If the water hits the blades from below, it is called an undershot water wheel. The horsepower furnished by water wheels is still used in some places to run various kinds of mill machinery.

Water pressure with the help of a mechanical device is used for lifting. Pumps and rams lift the water itself into tanks. Hydraulic jacks are used for lifting weights. The man at the service station uses a hydraulic jack to lift a car and hold it there while he changes a tire. The large piston holding up the car exerts much more pressure than the man uses to push down the handle of the jack.

Water went to work for us, too, with the invention of the steam engine. Steam, crowded in a boiler and pushing hard

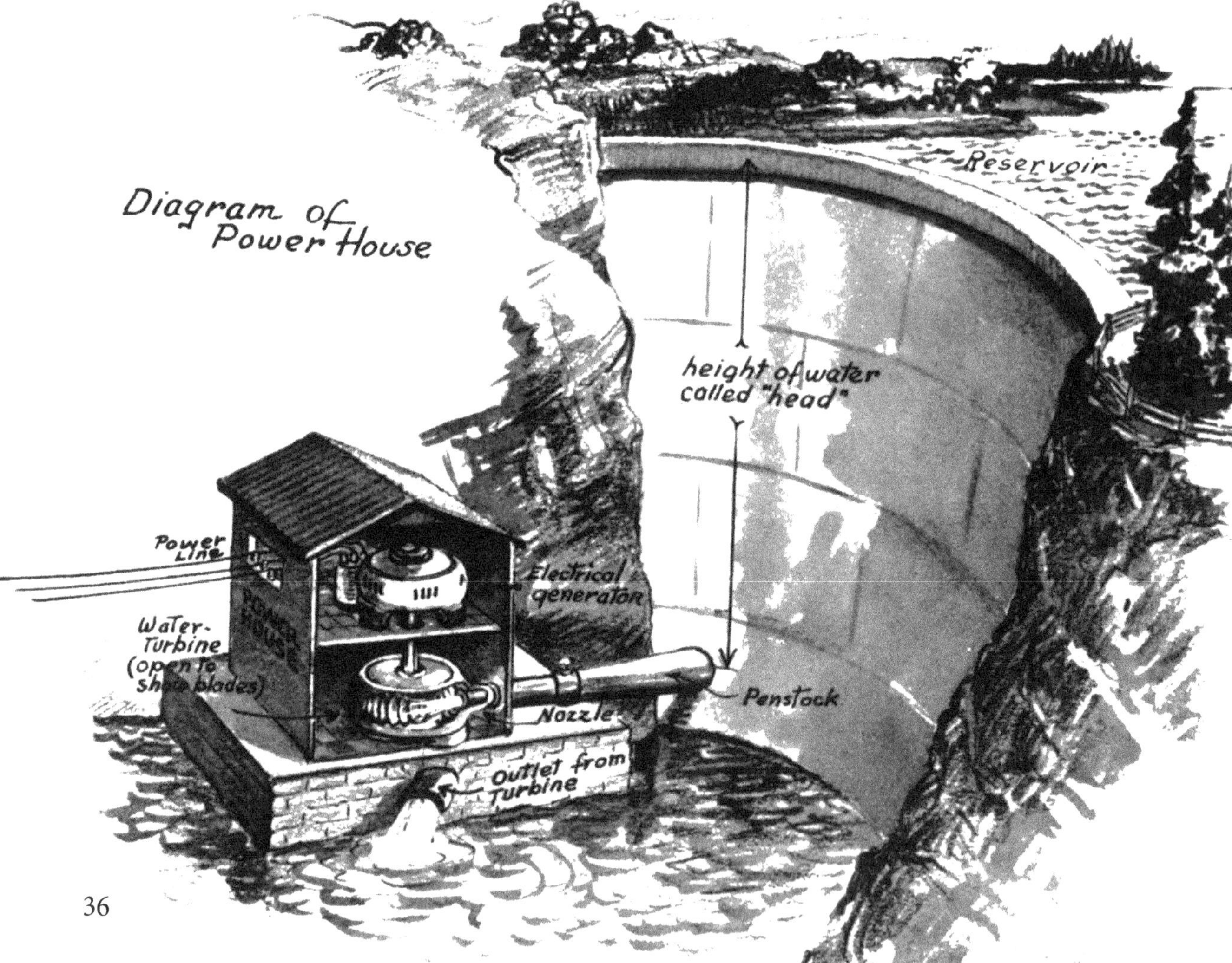

to get out of a small opening, furnishes a lot of energy. A steam engine does not need to be in a certain place, as a water wheel does, but can work anywhere if it has a boiler of water and fuel enough to keep the water boiling. It can even travel in the locomotive of a train or on an ocean-going ship.

Now we have electricity to give us light and power. From the powerhouse where it is generated, electricity travels on wires to where it is needed to drive our trains and transit buses and to work for us in factories and in homes. Generators of electricity are turned by steam, gasoline, or Diesel engines. They are also turned by water turbines.

A water turbine is a water wheel usually made so that it stands on end and spins like a top in a close-fitting case. Water spurts from a nozzle with great force against the blades of the turbine to keep it spinning. To get this great force, the water must be piped from a very high mountain lake or stream or from a high dam.

A small amount of water from a high lake can furnish as much power as a large amount of water from a low dam. The hydraulic engineers speak of "low head," "medium head," and "high head." Low heads are usually dams. High heads are pipes leading from as much as a mile up a mountain. The amount of water coming through a head is called the "flow."

The highest dams built are power dams. The Grand

VAPOR
CLOUDS
Fun in Water
THE STEAM ENGINE
② THE STEAM GOES THROUGH THIS PIPE AND INTO THE STEAM CHEST. FROM THERE IT IS DIRECTED INTO THE CYLINDER.
STEAM CHEST
SLIDE VALVE
(BELT RUNS MACHINERY)
CONNECTING ROD
FLY-WHEEL
① THE WATER IS HEATED IN THE BOILER AND BECOMES STEAM
PISTON
EXHAUST PIPE
③ THE STEAM PUSHES THE PISTON AND PISTON ROD. THESE IN TURN PUSH THE CONNECTING ROD WHICH TURNS THE CRANK OF THE FLYWHEEL.
④ WHEN THE FLYWHEEL HAS TURNED HALF W AROUND THE VALVE CHANGED ITS POSIT SO THE STEAM PUSHE PISTON BACK AGAIN USED STEAM (EX IS FORCED OUT
ECCENTRIC ROD
CROSS HEAD
PISTON ROD
CYLINDER
THE EXHAUST GOES "CHOO! CHOO! EACH TIME THE WHEEL
A WATER WHEEL
PIECES OF WOOD CU FROM AN APPLE BO

RAIN
SNOW
Fun on Ice
Fun in Snow
HOW A LIFT-PUMP WORKS
A SMALL STREAM
OR A GARDEN HOSE
TURNS THE WHEEL
1
PUSH THE HANDLE
DOWN AND THE
PLUNGER COMES
UP (LIKE A PISTON)
IT PUSHES THE AIR
OUT THROUGH THE
SPOUT. THE WATER
BELOW PUSHES
THE VALVE OPEN
AND FILLS THE
EMPTY SPACE BELOW
THE PLUNGER.
VALVE
WELL
2
LIFT THE HANDLE AND
THE PLUNGER GOES DOWN.
THE VALVE IN THE PLUNGER
IS PUSHED OPEN BY THE
WATER AS IT FLOWS THROUGH.
3
PUSH THE HANDLE
DOWN. UP COMES
THE WATER, OUT
INTO THE BUCKET.

Coulee Dam in the state of Washington is used for both irrigation and power. It is 550 feet high and over three-quarters of a mile long. It has enough flow to operate a row of eighteen turbines of 150,000 horsepower each. (One horsepower is the force necessary to lift 550 pounds one foot off the ground in one second.) The electricity generated at this dam can serve several cities and the surrounding country.

During the gold rush in Alaska, high heads were used in sluicing for gold. The miners used a big nozzle they called “The Hydraulic Giant.” The water came out of the nozzle with enough force to wash out whole hillsides where the gold was located.

A story is told of a man who made a bet that he could cut his cavalry sword through the stream where it came out of the big nozzle. Gripping his sword tightly, he slashed at the stream

with all his strength. The stream was hardly dented, but its force jerked the sword so violently that the man's shoulder was broken.

FROM CLOUDS, TO EARTH, TO AIR

That glass of water that you drew from the tap in your kitchen could have been a part of the working water that turned the blades of a great turbine. It could have been in a wave that splashed against your boat, or water left dripping from a log pushed up on the ocean beach at high tide.

It might even have been snow on a mountain, some of a beaver's pond, or in an iceberg where it had been frozen for a thousand years. It might have traveled great distances as water vapor, changing from cloud to cloud.

Now, today, it is handy here in your tap. You expect that there will be plenty of water there tomorrow and next year and for as many years as you want it, because that tap draws water from the great reservoirs of the earth!

The ocean is the largest reservoir of all. We float ships upon its surface, take shellfish from its beaches at low tide, and catch fish and whales from its depths. We send up weather balloons to find out what kind of weather is brewing over it. But whatever we do has no effect upon the ocean. It keeps on receiving the rivers from the land, and the sun and wind take the water back to the land in their own way.

We have no effect upon the icecap reservoirs, either. They push their glacial snouts into the ocean where chunks break off and float away. These icebergs may be small or they may be miles in length. They move where the ocean currents take them until finally they melt away and become a part of the ocean itself.

Cloud reservoirs, too, go their own way, riding on the winds and dropping rain when the air temperature forces them to. During many a dry season, men have watched clouds passing overhead in the sky and wished that they could do something to make those clouds rain. Now, flyers some-times drop dry ice into a rain cloud from above, hoping to cool and condense the cloud's vapor into waterdrops that have to fall. They call this "seeding the clouds."

We have more control over the reservoirs of the land. We connect waterways and turn streams into new channels. We build dikes to hold rivers within their banks so that they cannot overflow and flood our homes and farms. We build dams to hold back water, and build gates in the dams to let the water flow out as we wish. We lead water in pipes to wherever we need it and store it in man-made lakes and tanks.

All of these land waters are increased by the rain and snow that falls on the land around them, but many of them have their beginnings in the mountain forest reservoirs.

Snow may fall over as long a period as nine or ten months in some mountain forests, but the greatest amount falls in winter. Then it piles up higher and higher around the tall evergreen trees. The warmth of spring days starts melting it away, first from the lower slopes, then, as the days grow warmer, from the higher slopes and shady places. By late summer the main forest snows are melted, the days are hot, and there is little rain. The streams are low but still supplied with water.

Denny, who was camping in the mountain forest, wondered about this. He and his father followed a trail up the mountain river. Sometimes they found small streams joining the main river from upland lakes. More often they came upon under-ground water trickling from between layers of rock in the bank. The river dwindled smaller and smaller until finally Denny could step across it. Then it disappeared under a big snowbank.

"Why, it's melting right out from that snow!" Denny exclaimed. And there are more big snowfields above it!"

"It's a good thing that snow melts slowly here," Denny's father said. "If it all melted at once and when the lower forest snows melt, our rivers would really flood the country. Then they'd all dry up during the hot summer as they do now in some treeless regions. Trees help a lot. They shade the snowbanks so that the snow melts slowly. Their roots help hold back water, too, and keep the mountain soil from being washed away."

Denny's father stopped to read a sign nailed to a tree, "this is your national forest, keep it green. Even our government helps water do its work, by protecting the forests. From clouds to the earth, back to the air, that's the way water travels, but plants help keep it from traveling too fast. Water seems to play a very important part with sun and wind and earth and air—with everything in the world around us—all the time."

www.ingramcontent.com/pod-product-compliance
Ingram Content Group UK Ltd.
Pitfield, Milton Keynes, MK11 3LW, UK
UKHW062003290726
14090UKWH00022B/1372

9 781922 950680